This book belongs to:

T0343956

For Mum

First published 2024 by Walker Books Ltd
87 Vauxhall Walk, London SE11 5HJ

2 4 6 8 10 9 7 5 3 1

This book has been typeset in Avenir

Printed in China

British Library Cataloguing in Publication Data:
a catalogue record for this book is available from the British Library

ISBN 978-1-5295-0911-3

www.walker.co.uk

Oops!
Rabbit

WALKER BOOKS
AND SUBSIDIARIES
LONDON · BOSTON · SYDNEY · AUCKLAND

Jo Ham

Rabbit on

Oops!

Rabbit off

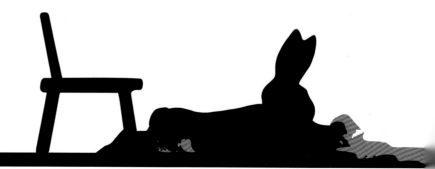

Rabbit on

Oops!

Rabbit off

Rabbit on

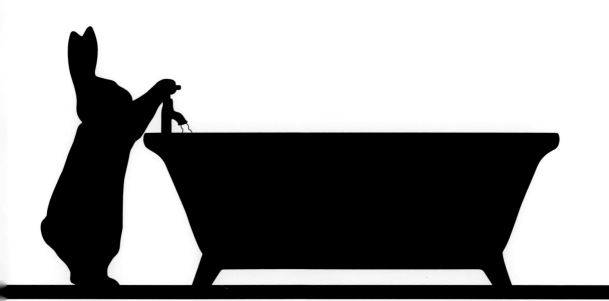

Rabbit off

Rabbit on

Rabbit ON!